April lives in New York with her dad.

The Kraang

robot

This is a Kraang. It lives in a robot.

Raphael

This is Raph. He is strong.

Leonardo

This is Leo. He wants to be the leader.

Before you read ...
Who is good and who is bad in this story?

New Words

What do these new words mean? Ask your teacher or use your dictionary.

fight

The boys are **fighting**.

city

It's a big **city**.

hit

Hit it!

fall

The cat is **falling**.

leader

She's the **leader**!

people

There are four **people**.

team

This **team** can run fast.

save

Please **save** me!

van

It's an old **van**.

'We're the good guys!'

We're the **good guys**!

strong

The man is **strong**!

What does the title *Rise of the Turtles* mean? Ask your teacher.

TEENAGE MUTANT NINJA TURTLES

RISE OF THE TURTLES

CHAPTER ONE
Up to the city

'We want to go up to the city!' says Donnie.

'Please ...' says Leo.

'OK,' says Splinter. 'You are big Turtles now.'

'Thank you, Sensei!' the Turtles shout.
They stand in front of Splinter.
'Be good,' he says, 'and do not talk to people.'

The Turtles go up to the city.
'Wow!' says Leo. 'This is New York.'
'It's cool!' says Mikey.

The four brothers walk in the city. They see
a pizza boy. The pizza boy sees the Turtles.
'They're green!' shouts the boy. 'I'm going!'

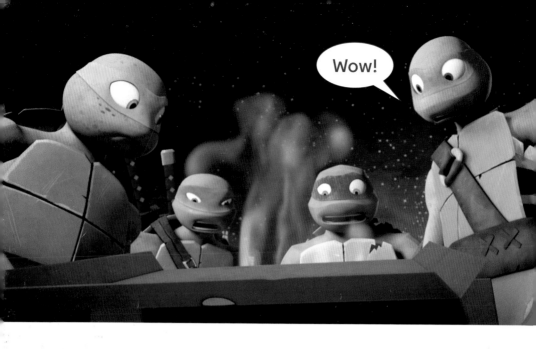

A pizza falls on the road.
'What is it?' asks Donnie.
'Can you eat it?' asks Leo.
Mikey eats some pizza. 'I love it!' he shouts.

The Turtles eat quickly.
'This is good!' says Raph.

CHAPTER TWO
'Let's save the girl!'

The Turtles are happy.

'I love this city!' shouts Mikey.

Suddenly, Donnie sees a girl. He stops.

'Look!' he says.

The girl's name is April. She is with her dad.

They are walking home. A van stops. Some men come out.

'Who are the men?' says Donnie.

The men stand in front of April and her dad.

'What do you want?' asks April's dad.

'Let's save the girl!' shouts Donnie.
'No!' says Leo. 'We don't talk to people.'
'I'm going!' says Donnie.
'Me too!' says Raph.
The Turtles go.

The Turtles fight the men, but the men are very strong.

'I'm fighting him!' shouts Raph.

'No, I want to fight him!' shouts Leo.

Donnie runs to save April. 'I've got you!' he says.

April sees Donnie. 'You're green!' she shouts.

'It's OK!' says Donnie. 'We're the good guys!'

Mikey is fighting a man.

'Stop!' shouts Donnie. 'I'm behind you!'

Now the man hits Donnie. Donnie and Mikey fall.

April and her dad are in the men's van.
'They've got the girl!' shouts Donnie.
'That's not good,' says Mikey.

Oh no!

CHAPTER THREE
'It's a robot!'

Raph, Leo and Donnie run after the van.
Mikey stands up slowly. There is one more
man in the road.

Mikey runs, but the man runs after him.
Mikey stops. He hits the man … and the
man falls.

'It's a robot!' says Mikey.

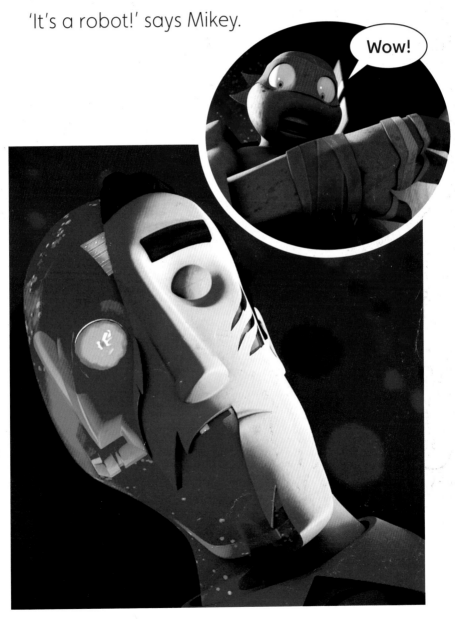

Wow!

A pink Kraang comes out of the robot and runs away.

'Aaaarrr!' shouts Mikey.

Mikey runs after his brothers.

'It's horrible and it's pink and it lives in a robot!' he shouts.

'What are you talking about?' says Leo. 'Let's go home.'

CHAPTER FOUR
'You are one team'

The Turtles talk to Splinter. 'The Kraang are bad guys,' says Leo.

Splinter is not happy. 'You are not strong, because you are not a team,' he says.

'We want to go up to the city again,' says Donnie. 'We want to save the girl.'

'Please ...' says Mikey.

'OK,' says Splinter. 'But you are not four turtles – you are one team.'

'Thank you, Sensei!' shout the Turtles.

'A team has a leader,' says Splinter.
'I want to be the leader!' says Leo
'No, I am!' says Raph.
'No, it's me!' say Donnie and Mikey.

'Your leader is Leonardo,' says Splinter.

'Let's go, Turtles!' says Leo. 'We're the good guys!'

THE END

WHAT'S UNDER

The Teenage Mutant Ninja Turtles live UNDER New York City. Do you know what is under your road?

manhole

Under a manhole

Do you have a manhole in your road? Where does it go? There is a very big pipe or sewer under the road. The water from your kitchen and bathroom goes into this sewer. Sewers are very big.

sewer

26

THE ROAD?

More pipes

There are pipes with clean water too. The clean water goes to your house. There are more pipes for gas.

Trains under your city

There are trains under some cities. There are about 190 cities in the world with underground trains. In Tokyo, in Japan, more than 8.5 million people go on the underground train every day.

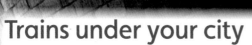
underground train

What's under your road? Make a list.

What do these words mean? Find out.
pipe   bathroom   clean   gas   every day

After you read

1 Match the questions and answers.

a) Who wants to go
up to New York?

i)

b) Who is a teacher?

ii)

c) Who lives in New York
with her dad?

iii)

d) Who lives in a robot?

iv)

2 Put the sentences in order. Write 1–6.

a) The Turtles eat pizza.　☐

b) A Kraang comes out of the robot.　☐

c) Donnie sees April.　☐

d) The Turtles go up to the city.　1

e) The Kraang have got April in the van.　☐

f) Donnie and Mikey fall.　☐

Where's the popcorn?
Look in your book.
Can you find it?

Puzzle time!

1 Solve the code and find the message.

20+3	0+5	9+9	3+2		15+5	4+4	4+1

W __ ' __ __   __ __ __

4+3	12+3	10+5	2+2		5+2	14+7	15+10	15+4

__ __ __ __   __ __ __ __!

Key:

D	E	G	H	O	R	S	T	U	W	Y
4	5	7	8	15	18	19	20	21	23	25

2 Choose the correct verbs in these sentences from the story.

1 A pizza **runs** / (**falls**) on the road.
2 We want to **fight** / **save** the girl.
3 Can you **eat** / **hit** it?
4 Do not **fight** / **talk to** people.

29

3 Write three sentences about the story.

		this story				bad.
I	like	the Kraang		it	is	funny.
We	don't like	Mikey	because	he	are	good.
		Raph		they		horrible.
		the Turtles				strong.

Example: I like Mikey because he is funny.

....

....

....

4 Which Turtle is this? Colour the letters in his name green. What do the letters in white spell? Draw it!

M	I	R	K	O	B	E	O	Y	T

Imagine...

Your teacher is going to read *Rise of the Turtles*. When the whistle blows, say the missing word.

For example:

Suddenly, Donnie sees a ♪

girl!

'Look!' he says. The girl's name is ♪

April!

Chant

1 Listen and read.

Under New York City

Under New York City
There's a big surprise,
Four turtle brothers
And they're the good guys!

Under New York City
They're strong and green,
Now Leo is the leader
They are a team!

2 T 8 9 Say the chant.

32